HOW TO [GET]

THAT

HIGHER

PAYING JOB

BY

BRUCE EDWARD BEAL

AN IMPRINT OF
ZWORLDNET PUBLISHING INC.
ISBN 0-9712310-9-5 //// A SPECIAL EDITION

HOW TO GET THAT

HIGHER

PAYING JOB

****

BY

BRUCE

EDWARD BEAL

****

****

****

**

ZWORLD-NET PUBLISHING INC.
PROUDLY PRESENTS

HOW TO GET
THAT
HIGHER
PAYING JOB

BY
BRUCE EDWARD BEAL

Finally,
The Holy Grail
of
Employment Books Has
Come!!!

PREFACE

This book is intended as an easy to read helpful guide to all those who want greater employment opportunities. Much of its content is a traditional application of good salesmanship to valid questions of a perspective employer. Additionally, a lot of great tried and proven tips are contained in this book that will help you achieve not only your employment goals but personal goals as well.

General attention is given, without specific guarantee, to many problems encountered by potential employees. It also addresses the problems of those desiring positions of upward mobility.

If you attend a traditional four-year institution, take advantage of your campus placement office. On campus facilities offer an array of job search preparations. These include: current job listings, resumes, and other job search assistances. For instance, an impressionable approach to a specific company may require a tailored resume. So, preparation of more than one resume is an advantage to you.

Students have the opportunity to consult a wide range of instructional and administrative talent and ultimately use their knowledge and counsel to determine current employment opportunities.

It is my sincere hope that you use this guide effectively and efficiently to your employment, and/or promotional success.

BRUCE EDWARD BEAL

Written in loving memory
of
Mrs. Inez Moreland.

**Special thanks also to
Mr. & Mrs. Wilmer "Buddy" Morris.**

This book was written by Bruce Edward Beal.

Initial Editing by:
Mrs. Nancy Perkins
Reconcilers Fellowship
Jackson, MS
And final edit by the award winning
ZWORLD-NET PUBLISHING STAFF

CHAPTER   **CONTENTS**   **PAGE**

Introduction.....................................10

1.   The First Presentation of Yourself......12

2.   Preparations...............................15

3.   Applications and Resumes...............20

4.   The Chronological Resume...............25

5.   The Functional Resume..................28

6.   Cover Letter Of Application.................30

7.   Cover Letter Of Inquiry...................33

8.   Request for Interview.....................36

9.   The Internet................................39

10.   The Interview..............................41

11.   Body Language.............................45

      A. Attire

      B. Eyes

      C. Limbs

12.   Blowing Your Own Horn.................49

13.   Using Your Local Library..............53

14.   Dealing With Rejection..................55

15.   Networking.............................58

16.   Roulette Calls.........................60

17.   Talking Shop...........................62

18.   Climbing the Corporate Ladder..........64

19.   Company Social Functions...............69

20.   Strategic Questions You Can Ask........72

21.   Tough Questions Asked by Employers..74

22.   Action Words to Protect You............80

23.   The Resume Record......................84

HOW TO GET
THAT
HIGHER
PAYING JOB

****

BY
BRUCE
EDWARD BEAL

****

Finally, the Holy Grail of employment
books has come!!!!

Your search is over

Read, and be enlightened!

INTRODUCTION

While considering various positions that might be available in conjunction with individual qualifications, many people rule themselves "unqualified" for jobs they are perfectly capable of handling. Fear, depression, and/or anxiety can generate within us a lack of confidence and the feeling that we can't qualify for a more authoritative position.

A winner knows a little about and most of all has confidence in the fact that her/she can win. A winner uses the totality of experience to get what he/she wants. The odds are sized up and then he goes for the jackpot. In this case, a specific job is the jackpot. Your qualifications and ability to manipulate are circumstantial odds. All related experience is invaluable.

In other words, when you actually **get down to it**, this is all about winning. "I am in competition with someone else for something we both want, and are probably equally qualified for. **I only have to figure how to win before my competition does."** The determining factor is, which of us has that winner's instinct.

In finding out the characteristics and qualifications of a job, count yourself in if you have had any experience in any phase of what the position calls for. On previous jobs, you may have had the responsibility of carrying out aspects of the job that were not included in the job description. These were valuable services, without which, the job would not have gone as smoothly as it did. Most companies have a training and/or probationary period which is usually ample time to learn the new routine, and/or develop an expertise of the job.

A good place to try your wings at winning is in the newspaper classifieds. The best offers are in the early editions of the Sunday and Monday newspapers. National magazines, the internet, and circulars are good sources of information, especially if you are interested in relocation.

If an employment agency is involved, an early morning start is emphasized; also more listings are available on Mondays. Later you will find that even the telephone book and the vast internet is valuable in your search for that Higher **Paying Job. Decide what you want and go after it.**

CHAPTER ONE

THE FIRST
REPRESENTATION
OF
YOURSELF

After deciding what you want, the first impression you give of yourself **is critically important**. It usually occurs in a phone call to the Personnel Director. Besides giving your name and asking about the availability of the position, be prepared to say why their ad caught your eye. Here is where you want to immediately start standing out in the crowd. Rehearse your conversation for briefness, getting to the point and to give an indication of your genuine interest.

An elaborate speech might make you sound phony. You need only to tentatively introduce yourself and ultimately arrange for an interview. You also want to inspire the Personnel Director's interest in you as a potential employee, And if possible make him or her eager to know more of your qualifications for the job.

Evaluating several positions simultaneously **does not make you a traitor to any particular company.** However, the last thing you want to do is give the impression that you are frantic from so much looking, and will take anything that offers more money. Keep an accurate account of times of interviews and names of personnel directors. It is good to have more than one option but remember, you are making the inquiry because you want to work for "that specific company."

Many people will give up in frustration at the initial call to the secretary's office without realizing that sometimes part of the secretary's job is to do a prescreen of you. The secretary could be your first challenge in the test of your perseverance and stamina. **Games may be played!** Don't be denied! Be tenacious! Just how badly do you want the job and to what extent will you go to accomplish your goal may be what is needed. Employers like to feel that their employees will not give up at the first sign of difficulty. Many employers will ask their secretaries after an encounter, **"Was the applicant persistent and DID HE sound hungry?"**

If you are told the personnel director is in conference, out of the office, or indisposed, **IT MAY AGAIN BE A TEST!** Be determined! Ask when he or she might be available to speak with you. It is acceptable to let the secretary know the subject matter in general; however, when it comes to answers you want them from the horse's mouth and not a subordinate. **There is no reason to become arrogant. This could do more harm than good.** If you are arrogant or bothersome as a prospective employee, you might continue with that after employment. So take heed of this valuable advise. **A little persistence however, sometimes pays a lot.**

CHAPTER TWO

PREPARATIONS

Have a friend or relative give you an interview (what is called a mock interview) using the questions at the end of this booklet. (See Questions, STARTING at page 74). Do your homework and thoroughly research the job you are seeking. Compose mock interview questions specific to the jobs you are seeking that the perspective employer might just ask you, as well.

You can best observe your mannerism by reviewing tapes made by camcorder. If you have access to one, even through a friend or relative, you will probably find them willing to help you. If a camcorder is not available, practice your mannerism in a full-length mirror.

Strive to maintain a **POSITIVE** and **PROGRESSIVE** attitude about yourself. Your demeanor should be confident and relaxed. Prepare to energetically discuss your past achievements, and job related experiences; and how you, as an asset, could contribute to the company.

It is an important and an added incentive to the employer, if you list your hobbies; community and volunteer work; affiliated organizations; and membership. **All work and no play makes Jack a dull boy. The potential employer is trying to form an overall picture of your general character. If you don't do anything on your own time, you might not do anything on someone else's time either.** No employer wants to have the slightest indication that he or she could pay you for eight hours of work, and have you give less than that in productivity.

In listing references, the crony system is good; but get some straight talk from those you list that are already within the company. If your friend has worked for the company for a while, it is quite possible that he or she has accumulated enemies from within. If so, you want to know who, as you would not want to list company enemy number one.

Many of us are in the situation of working one job while attempting to acquire another. "Progress time" is the key issue here. It is perfectly normal to arrange an interview after working hours. Just explain that your present job does not allow for other interviews.

In a case of traveling to another city, elicit inquiries before your trip. Schedule your interviews accordingly, from as early as 7 a.m. until evening, you can arrange productive interviews. **We suggest no more than three.**

Unless your campaign is perfectly orchestrated, it is inadvisable to let your present employer become knowledgeable of your efforts. A search for your replacement could go out. Explain to your superiors how you speak of your company's progress and your responsibility in doing your share to maintain that progress. Inquires of your availability to another company is a moot subject.

We should stipulate here that you should not quit your present job and go off "in search of" another one or pie in the sky as it is commonly called! This is never wise. Even if you have to use vacation time for this purpose, you are more valuable as a working individual.

At this point, it is imperative that you understand your immediate objectives--**SALES**! You want to **SELL** yourself and your talent to the perspective employer. It is important that you present your abilities and personality as a viable commodity and service. A service which the perspective employer is willing to buy.

You should have already accessible not less than three reliable references. They should have knowledge of your background and of your immediate efforts to seek gainful employment.

High school students entering the job market should consult their school counselors. They can advise you on tentative career opportunities. In many cases they have knowledge of immediate job openings, internships and scholastic programs.

Students enrolled in Junior and Technical colleges have variable avenues to potential employment. You might not have designated job counselors within your school. However, in many instances, your instructional staff is willing to assist you.

If you attend a traditional four-year institution, take advantage of your campus placement office. On campus facilities offer an array of job search preparations. These include: current job listings, resumes, and other job search assistances. For instance, an impressionable approach to a specific company may require a tailored resume. So, preparation of more than one resume is an advantage to you.

Students have the opportunity to consult a wide range of instructional and administrative talent. Use their knowledge and counsel to determine current employment opportunities.

*Directional needs of other employment searchers will be addressed within this presentation.

CHAPTER THREE

APPLICATIONS AND RESUMES

By this time you have recognized the importance of proper preparations. In filling out applications and resumes, you should be concise, descriptive and as summative as possible. Frequent use of appropriate punctuation is valuable here. For instance: Laboratory technician (8/5/78-11/6/79).

Duties and Responsibilities: Phlebotomy; arterial blood-gas analysis; inventory of supplies; evaluation for specific improvements…etc.

In preparing this written representation of yourself, take note of the fact that this record is the only thing speaking on your behalf for the moment. It is critically important that you be very impressive at this point in time! Your resume And its format should be consistent, neat and typewritten for best results. Many companies require an application along with a resume. If so, try to obtain an application before hand and fill it out under comfortable circumstances. Again, a typewritten resume says more of your sense of organization, and quality of character. If typing is not an option, neatly printed dark ink is acceptable.

Don't hesitate to record every job related experience, responsibility and/or duty carried out by you and especially those relevant to the sought after position.

Most employers know that many times the little added attention to details that an employee is willing to give is essential to the progress of the company. This may give you, as an applicant, the winner's edge over your competition. Try to address all questions and if something doesn't apply to you, either write or type in a small horizontal slash mark in the answer space provided.

If there is something that you simply would prefer to leave blank, explain that you did not know who was going to see the application, and feel you could explain it better in person. Some matters are handled best when kept between the employer and employee.

A functional resume is to your advantage here. However, it is the responsibility of the applicant to explain any period of job inactivity. Prepare yourself to do this, In general a resume consist of: a Heading, an Employment Objective or Summary of your Educational Experience and Work History. The order of this outline is not written in stone; however, there are variable formats.

Currently there are two resume formats accustomed by the corporate world. These are the Chronological and Functional resumes. In some instances you might want to combine these two formats. Each format should be accompanied by an introductory cover letter.

The Chronological Resume displays your work history in descending order, or starting with the last job you held. It places emphasis on the dates and time spans of your educational and job endeavor. Younger candidates are encouraged to use this format in that it presents a cohesive idea of your educational and work histories.

The Functional Resume encompasses an array of skills concurrent to one's job title. It emphasizes the job capacity in which one has served: Managing Editor, Medical Technologist. The design of this resume is lenient to an older candidate with periods of job inactivity.

As stated earlier, prepare yourself to explain these periods. By now, my best attribute should be, "my problem solving ability."

An effective cover letter will enhance your probability to secure a job interview. This document is your introduction to the potential employer, and is a corroboration of your resume.   Your first objective is to compel the resume screener to pay special attention to your credentials.

This is the best accomplished by a solid opening statement. Immediately show that, "I am forthright in my sense of thought, positive in my direction and confident in my ability." Adequately describe your attributes. (See actions words)

In general, you should state the position desired, your learned skills and their qualifications, your knowledge of the company and your plans to become an asset to the company when you are
hired. If you are unfamiliar with a company, you might use an exploratory inquisition letter.

All business letters are neatly typed and single spaced.   And as with your resume, this document will not tolerate errors. Each of these documents should consist of no more than one double-spaced typed page. The reader is advised to examine several resumes and their formats. Choose the one that will convey an enhancing concept of your talent, experience and career potential. You can find varied formats in your college career placement office and in your local library.

If you do not own or have access to a computer, there are agencies that will prepare your resume for a fee. Many of these services are listed in the produce service index of your local telephone directory. You may also find them in the classified section of your local newspaper. The reader is advised to shop for quality as well as price.

CHAPTER FOUR

Sample Resume Formats
(The chronological style)

The following format illustrates the recommended form and content for your resume. The use of indentation, underlining and broad headings allows the employer to make an initial evaluation of your credentials in relation to specific job openings in a short amount of time. For example.

YOUR NAME

PRESENT ADDRESS / PERMANENT ADDRESS
Street   / Street
City, State, Zip Code   / City, State, Zip Code

PROFESSIONAL OBJECTIVE:

Describe the type of work yo u
desire, both on a short-range
and on a long-range basis. The
words "career" or "job" may
be substituted for "profession."

EDUCATION:

Present highest degree data
first, and work backward.
Identify: major, minor, courses
of study, institution granting
degree and date of graduation.

EXPERIENCE   (DATE)

Identify employer, your title
and a brief description of the
duties performed. Start with
the most recent employment
and record data in reverse
chronological order.

(DATE)

Include volunteer work if it is
related to the professional
objective. Also include
summer jobs of significant
duration and importance.

HONORS AND ACTIVITIES:

Include clubs, organizations,
and honor societies. If and
officer, specify which office.

INTEREST:

Special skills and hobbies;
travel, knowledge of other
countries, language, etc.

MILITARY SEVICE:

If applicable, include the
branch of service, dates of
service, rate or rank, and

JOB EXPERIENCE:

Summarize your job
experience. Prioritize them
as they relate to the job in
which you are now applying.

REFERENCES:

State that references are
available upon request.

AVAILABILITY DATE:

Give a reasonable time that
You will be ready to start.

CHAPTER FIVE

Sample Resume Formats
(THE FUNCTIONAL STYLE)

The following is an example of the functional style.

Itasha Moreland
1219 East Arbor Drive
Jackson, Tennessee 46339
(312) xxx-5369

Summary:

Administrative Manager with B.S. in Economics and M.B.A. thesis in progress. Fifteen years' professional experience with increasing responsibility in purchasing, management and cost analysis.

Experience and Accomplishments:

Warehouse Manager,
Mahogany Farms and Produce
Spartenberg, MS
1985 – Present

Duties: Determining market trends in produce, labor availability and company shipping costs. Managed staff of fifteen to secure planned shipment of perishable goods, document inventory, initiate plans to modernize transport equipment and supplies. Massive restructuring of company truck routes stream-line costs. Reduces fuel and weight load expenditures $273,000 annually.

1979-84
Shipping and receiving Clerk I. Assumed position of Interim Warehouse Manager; formally promoted in 1981.

Supervised staff of fourteen to document and disperse department store merchandise to proper store site. Annual merchandise flow rate $16,000,000. Initiated and implemented systems XI-II-D (Computer Scan) for monitoring of merchandise. Attained annual savings to company, $426,000.

Education: Pemberton State University, Pemberton, Ms. M.B.A. program, 1994-present, part-time. Anticipated completion date: May 1995. Mount Angelo College, Blue Hill, TN. B.S. in Economics, Who's Who in American Colleges and Universities, with 3.9 G.P.A. upon graduation. Gamma Phi Honor Society.

Reference: Furnished upon request.

CHAPTER SIX

COVER LETTER OF APPLICATION

Use this letter when you are applying for a job you saw listed or one you know is open and available. Follow the style and organization suggested but choose words and ideas that portray your identity. Proofread for errors. However, if you are not good at writing, get help with spelling and structure.

Your Present Address
City, State, Zip Code

Date of Letter
Individual's Name
Title
Employer
Street Address
City, State, Zip Code

Dear _____: (Use
name, never, "To Whom it may concern" etc.")

Opening Paragraph:

State why you are writing. Identify the position by
name, state that you wish to apply for the position;
mention where and when you saw or heard about
the job described.

Middle Paragraph:

One or two middle paragraphs should tell the reader
about your best qualifications and credentials. Pick
the one or two things about your training, your
personal assets, your achievements that directly
relate to the skills needed in the sought-after job.

Closing Paragraphs:

Make it easy for the employer to respond to your
wishes. Your main goal in this letter is to get a
personal interview.

Local Employer:

Directly state your desire for a personal interview.
Give the reader any information that will make it
easier to contact you for the interview. Be positive
and enthusiastic.

Long Distance Employer:

state specifically the dates you will be in the area. Ask for an interview. You may suggest a date and time.

Sincerely,

(your handwritten signature)

Type Your Name

Enclosure (resume, application, etc.)

CHAPTER SEVEN

COVER LETTER OF INQUIRY

Use this letter when you are making a general inquiry about possible vacancies. Follow the style and organization suggested but, choose words and ideas that portray your identity. Proofread for errors. If you are not good at writing, get help with spelling and structure.

> Your Present Address
> City, State, Zip Code

Date of Letter
Individual's Name
Title
Employer
Street Address
City, State, Zip Code

Dear _____: (Use
name, never "To Whom it may concern" etc.")

Opening Paragraph:

Indicate your reason for writing, which is to make a
general inquiry about possible job vacancies.

Middle Paragraphs:

One or two middle paragraphs should tell the
reader about your best qualifications and
credentials. Pick the one or two things about your
training, your personal assets, your achievements
that would best fit the skills needed for an
imagined position at this company.

Closing Paragraph:

Make it easy for the employer to respond to your
wishes. Your main goal in this letter is to get a
personal interview.

Local Employer:

State directly your desire for a personal interview.
Give the reader any information that will make it
easier to contact you for the interview. Be positive
and enthusiastic.

Long Distance Employer:

State specifically the dates you will be in the area.
Ask for an interview. You can suggest a date and
time.

Sincerely,

(your handwritten signature)

Type Your Name

Enclosure (resume, application, etc.)

CHAPTER EIGHT

REQUEST FOR AN INFORMATIONAL INTERVIEW

This kind of letter facilitates the exploratory interview and is useful in contacting "targets" in your search within the "hidden" job market. It avoids mention of "jobs" or "interviews," focusing instead on your desire for information, advice, help, exploration of careers and jobs. Using this approach, you can get in to see almost anyone you wish. Do not use this format when applying for a listed job.

Your Present Address
City, State, Zip Code

Date of Letter

Individual's Name
Title
Employer
Street Address

City, State. Zip Code

Dear _____: (Use name, never "To Whom it may concern" etc.")

Opening Paragraph:

Explain your career interest; that you are pursuing or exploring a career in _____. Ask the reader to share insights, experience, advice in this field. Mainly, that you need more information about the career or that you need the advice of an expert and would like the reader's reactions to your ideas and perspective in the field. Mention, you are asking the reader to spend a brief period of time with you, talking about a field of mutual interest. Ask for an "appointment," not an interview.

Middle paragraphs:

Devote one or two paragraphs to making positive statements about yourself. Summarize your best qualifications. You want to give the reader an idea of your interests, so your forthcoming discussion can be more fruitful. Focus on job goals, achievements, educational background, experience, professional skills. Mention that you are enclosing a resume so that the reader can gain an overview of your background and interests.

Closing paragraph:

Re-state your eagerness for advice and help.

Local Inquiry:

Tell the reader you will phone a few days in advance to schedule a personal appointment. (Do not call it an interview.)

Long Distance Employer:

If you are doing a long distance job search, tell the reader when you are planning to be in the area and ask for a reply listing a convenient appointment time. Tell the reader you are anticipating a busy schedule when you are in town and would appreciate establishing an appointment by (give a deadline). Mention that if you have not heard from the reader, you will phone the first day you are in town to arrange an appointment.

Sincerely,

(your handwritten signature)

Type Your Name

Enclosure

CHAPTER NINE

THE
INTERNET

(Video Resumes)

An innovative approach to exhibit one's talent is through the Internet System. This method is not for everyone, in that, to display only a standard resume would inadequately serve our purpose here. *(U.S. News and World Report October 1994.)* However an applicant with the appropriate background could benefit by using this medium.

Some areas might include various aspects of computers, engineering and fine arts. Here we are using the law of probability but with an integral twist. The greater number of potential employers you contact, the probability to acquire a job interview is improved. Many job listings are also posted. The internet enable you to amplify contacts.

The reader is advised that a visual presentation of yourself and your talent requires cohesive precision. It is essential that you display an appropriate audiovisual, editing, and graphics format. These aspects of your presentation are pivotal to your success or failure in getting a job interview. "I will need assistance." Instructional computer software is available to help you. Consult your library for companies that provide this service.

This method of job search could become lucrative in terms of positive feedback. However, it can become time consuming and costly as well. At this writing there is little documentation on the success rate of this method.

One should **also not over look the many sites available on the internet to look for employment.** You can launch your resume to very productive sites such as Monster.com. There are also many government employment websites such as USAjobs.com that you can strategically place your resume. Additionally, many of the larger companies not only utilize internet web sites but also insist that your initial contact with them be through this method. Don't be shy! Send as many resumes as possible, one to each potential employer. The internet will save you a lot of shoe leather!

Remember, you may only get one chance via the internet to make a great impression, so make absolutely certain that you put your best foot forward. Your resume should be nothing short of outstanding.

CHAPTER TEN

THE
INTERVIEW

What you want to do here is to get onto the same frequency as the employer of personnel director, so preparations should be made in this area. If you've not worked in a desired field for a while, read and learn some of the current terminology of lingo of that discipline. Look for the opportunity to bring your current knowledge into the discussion when you have your interview.

Your knowledge will not do you any good if the perspective employer isn't aware of that knowledge. Be careful, however, not to work yourself into the position of implying you know something, which could lead to an elaborate discussion of something you know nothing about.

Know your weaknesses. Prepare to make improvements. Do what ever it takes to get the job done. Some of those critical brush-ups can be acquired through current magazines. If more in depth study is required, a trip to the local library can only help. You might state this as an occasional hobby.

It also helps to know something about the overall production of the company of service you are interested in. In most cases, an employer feels good that you have interest enough to watch the developments of the company. A team player, which you will become when you get the job, is knowledgeable and aware of circumstances that could affect production.

The less the employer feels you have to be told about the specifics of the operation, the more he or she feels assured that you will blend in well with the company operation, and its present employees. Most companies and services have brochures which explain their system of doing things. Obtain and familiarize yourself with its contents. This information will be valuable from another aspect, as will be discussed later.

During the interview, one should prepare to give a **short** and **concise** response to **ANYTHING.** In order to get to know the "real you," some personnel directors will talk of everything but subjects pertaining to job-related experiences. These might range from something you listed as a hobby, to your knowledge and feelings of perceptual concept in aero dynamic design.

Above all else, appropriately answer the question asked of you. Remember you are doing this for that position of authority, stability and higher pay. Immediate concentration and response will give you a tremendous advantage in presenting an appropriate portrait of yourself.

Employers, many times, are more persistent in pursuing questions not answers by the perspective employee than those answered. For example, why did you find those courses appealing? Or did you have to study very hard? In the course of taking interviews, there are a few standard questions you can expect. These, in part include areas such as your long-range career objectives; what you expect to be earning in five or ten years; how would you describe yourself; and some will ask directly... **why should I hire you?**

Above all else, appropriately answer the question asked of you "**Because I'm very good in my progression and I strive for excellence at all times.**"

A former colleague was asked by his interview screener, "can you take an order?" Taking and executing an order is crucial to the overall function of an organizational effort, can **YOU** give one, "he added?

In general, you can look for the employer to probe your abilities in:

A. Leadership qualities.
B. Maturity.
C. Planning and Organizations.
D. Ability to get along with people.
E. Technical Competence.
F. Personal Motivation.
G. Stability on choice of career.

CHAPTER ELEVEN

BODY LANGUAGE

A. EYES

Ever heard the expression that "the eyes are the mirror to the soul?"   While having your interview, maintain eye contact. Even if you have only a quaint one, remember **smile,** you're on stage. Looking around the room or down at the floor while answering certain questions can place doubt in the employer's mind concerning your answers.

Many of us have bent or broken the rules of society. If you are, and have, repent. You can look society in the eye again. This interview is your new start to do so.

Eye contact is suggestive of your sincerity. If interviewed by a panel, direct your answers to the group as a whole.   For best results in this situation, speak directly to specific members of the panel on occasion. **Don't underestimate anyone's significance or importance.** Your future supervisor could be there. If you have a serious problem with stage fright, as many people do, **a little trick** is to look at the lower middle forehead of the individual being addressed. Before focusing entirely on that person, calmly move your eyes along to other individuals in the room.

B. ATTIRE

Since you have now probably eliminated those positions unworthy of your talents, and/or below your financial goals, it's time to tune up your fine points, some of which you may not be aware. A **crisp suit of clothes that need not be expensive**, elaborate or fancy, will do a lot for yourself-confidence. If, however you are in the world of high fashion modeling, prepare to show how elaborate and most of all, how versatile you can look. This is accomplished with an appropriate portfolio.

You feel good when you look good , and you want to look up-to-date and on the ball. A little shine on the shoes and a bit of attention to the fingernails helps enhance that first impression.

Gentlemen, remember--a dark suit and tie with tasteful apparel works best.

Ladies usually inspire more confidence in themselves, by observing a moderately conservative dress code.

Avoid overly flashy costumes and colors. The lady's corporate business jacket can be quite effective for your purpose here. The neck should be tastefully adorned. However, you do not want to look gaudy.

Your shoes should reflect your sense of neatness as well as coordination, and they should appropriately cover your entire foot.

A good pair of seamless nylon hose! Now, you are ready! You are dressed for success! Consider yourself dressed to your confident best.

C. LIMBS

Have you ever observed a cross-examination and the witness folds his arms after being asked a certain question? A good attorney usually interrogates rigorously after such an exhibition. In this situation, the witness is suggestive of psychologically holding something in that he/she doesn't want to come out. Be mindful of such actions, as they might suggest that you are unnecessarily on the defensive about something.

Over-exaggerated hand motions might indicate inadequate communication skills, or difficulty in explaining a specific matter. The hands are appropriate for emphasis in some cases, however, do not become frantic with it. Place your feet flat on the floor, your arms on the rest of the chair and let the employer know that your cards are on the table.

Ladies, legs can be crossed appropriately at the ankles, bent underneath the chair. You're ready for a fully, open and honest examination.

CHAPTER TWELVE

BLOWING
YOUR OWN HORN
TACTFULLY

When applying for a position, **the first thing you have to do is sell your skills.** Use your mouth; it's the most persuasive tool you have in this situation. In acquiring any position, one has to sell him or herself to the employer. This should be done with the calmness of a five-star general.

As stipulated earlier, the conversational range is not to be confined. **One should be assertive and positive about the past, and stable about the future.** In terms of opinions, it is good to have definitive convictions; however, it is best to explain your position from a moderate point of view without emotional duress. Even if you have a strong conviction on a particular issue, certain blandness of facial expression and voice tone helps to neutralize a negative judgment of your opinion.

Keep in mind that the employer is intent to hire a "character" that can be shaped along with that of the company.

Some people feel badly at times about blowing their own horns. Nobody wants to be thought of as a braggart. After all, most braggarts are quite fragile in their reflections of past accomplishments. **But if there ever was a time for bragging, this is it. If you don't tell the employer of your accomplishments, nobody else is going to do it for you.**

You can't put every good memory and personal sense of accomplishment onto your application or resume. If you catered or cooked for a fabulous affair at a swank dinner party, an applicant for Head Chef should recall and relate the affair. If you can drop the appropriate name, it's quite healthy for your promotional efforts.

When the employer is finished questioning you, invariably you will be given the opportunity to ask questions that may be on your mind. Here is where having read those brochures will come in handy. Ask specific questions that were not answered by the interviewer, and/or the brochure. Do not put the interviewer on the defensive, however, you may have unanswered questions.

Prepare as many questions as you can in advance of your interview. (See questions, p. 74.) Impel the interviewer to cater to your enthusiasm, and interest in the company. Good points to explore are those of retirement plans; possible profit sharing; medical benefits; and naturally, opportunity for advancement.

If you can compel within the interviewer the need to impress you with the performance of the company, the ballgame is in your favor. However, don't appear haughty or above the company's operation. Show your approval by agreement with the past accomplishments or positive directions of the company.

Upon closing your interview you want to be positive and on the up-beat. If you only say "thank you for your time," you might as well add, "and so much for that." Ask when will you expect to hear something from the potential employer.

Upon receiving the response, further inquire "is it all right if I give you a call if I don't hear from you by that time." These are final clinches that further substantiate your assertiveness, and determination. Wish the potential employer a good day, and re-state that you look forward to hearing something from him or her.

If you feel that you did not do as well in your interview as you wanted to, it's still not gloom and doom. You can impact after the fact. This involves waiting until the set deadline in which you are to receive your response. Make several calls to the office and inquire as to the decision. This can be quite effective in presenting an encore presentation of yourself.

Your objective here is to encourage the association of your name every time the employer thinks of the position you are trying to secure. To enhance this process, send a thank you card to your interview screener immediately following your interview.

It has been said, **"Whoever invented work didn't finish the job."** If and when your job seeking machinery is well in place, maintain a state of readiness, especially just prior to and on holidays. An employer will contact you one day, even on holidays, asking you, "when can you come to work?" **Your answer should be something similar to..."Is right now too late?"**

CHAPTER THIRTEEN

USING YOUR
LOCAL LIBRARY
(OH SO EFFECTIVELY!)

Until recently, **the public library has been a vastly under-used** source of opportunity in job sought information. As far your success is concerned, you're going to change this and from now on use this invaluable tool to achieve your career success! Within this one facility, you will find a wealth of company listings, complete with street addresses. Many attractive career opportunities are also available. Accessing this information will enable you to confine, and target your job search efforts. Concentrate on areas where your chances for career success are heightened, and are within the disciplines of your expertise.

In most library facilities, much of the afore mentioned information is neatly computerized. You will also find "job ad" listings, from newspapers published out of town. And, in many cases, nationwide.

Specific information on resume preparation is also available; and, it is all free of charge. You need only to dust off the old library card, or acquire a new one. Within the public library, a good place to start might be the magazine and/or newspaper room. If you need help, as many of us do, just ask the "attendant in charge." You'll find the employees professionally informative, and willing to assist you in a cordial manner. **GO FOR IT.**

Your local state-run employment agency is available with an abundance of job listings. The best "pickings" are usually early on Monday mornings. Adhere to caution, if you plan to use a private or commissioned-based employment service. Thoroughly investigate the agency's: credentials, policies, and credibility. When a job is found for you, the employer may require a "probation period." If you fail the company's probation requirements, and lose the job, you will still have a financial obligation to the job agency.

CHAPTER FOURTEEN

DEALING WITH
REJECTION

Rejection, unfortunately, is an integral fact of life. Although this book will prepare you to be at your best, statistics show that most contacts to get a job from an employer will fail. You must be aware of this fact and be prepared when it happen to pick yourself up, brush yourself off and continue on to the next interview with a smile.   You can be confident that with the tools provided in this book, you will get that HIGHER paying job. This book will give you the best chance to succeed in the least amount of time possible.

This positive attitude and confidence will be your shield against the ugly crippling beast known as rejection.   It will give you what you need to continue to surge forward when all others about you fall. You will be able to recover from rejection's terrible sting. This positive attitude and approach to handling rejection will ultimately help my readers achieve their goals.

Since our earliest stages of postnatal existence, we have all encountered this reaction. If you have not done so in the past, **now is the time to deal with it effectively.**

Infants cry for a variety of reasons. They have the need for food, warmth, affection, etc. When a parent cannot respond to the infant's specific need, is this rejection of the infant's need, by the parent? There may be other variables involved. Of course, the parent wishes to satisfy the infant, and stop it's crying. The previously mentioned scenario is not rejection. It is a failure in communication. The infant cannot communicate in the language accustomed to the parent.

In your interview with a perspective employer, make certain that you communicate your abilities clearly, and concisely. Refrain from using phrases that begin with, "ah…you know, like u-h-h."

A good salesperson knows that not every negotiation will come to a successful conclusion. However, the salesperson will make adjustments in his or her sales approach and "hit the ground running" again and again. This is done with pleasant, positive, and upbeat disposition.

Upon each job interview appointment you receive, certain factors should become apparent. "The probability of getting the job is now in my favor. I have already achieved a status that many of my competitors did not achieve. I will make the most of my job interview, while the situation exists. I'm now, "one up."

One should develop the above state of mind when looking for employment. It is essential that a job seeker maintain a sense of stamina, perseverance, and determination.

CHAPTER FIFTEEN

NETWORKING

(SOMETIMES WHO YOU KNOW CAN GET YOU WHERE YOU WANT TO BE)

Hum, "who do I know with the capacity to further develop my network of job contacts? You may ask yourself. A former schoolmate or social acquaintance might have the influence to propel your name to the top of the hiring list. Just make sure that your credentials are in order when this valuable opportunity presents itself.

Arrange a meeting with this "valuable" friend. Tentatively explain your situation, and make adjustments for possible conflicts in schedules. In this meeting, make an implicit point that you are seeking employment. Do not exacerbate the issue, after all, this is your old friend. With good eye to eye contact, tactfully infuse your talent and work experience into the conversation. Listen for appropriate feedback.

Upon nearing the end of your meeting you should have received sufficient information. If not, ask your questions in a more direct manner. "My goal here is to locate job openings in various companies, institutions and establishments. I will need the names of contact persons and their department."

Ask your friend if you may use his or her name as a follow through reference. Obtain a candid understanding on any matter that could be construed, or labeled as an official indiscretion on your part. "I am now impending my friend's reputation and I will not compromise it". Follow up on all leads **immediately!!**

This effort is sometimes labeled cronyism or nepotism, in the case of a relative. However when talents meet the job requirements, it is labeled "gainfully Employed."

CHAPTER SIXTEEN

Roulette Calls

For those of you who might be bummed out to the point of not having enough available sources in which to apply your skills, this is a good place to start. **We should state here that this method is not an easy one. However, it can be effective in terms of scheduling a possible interview.** Since most businesses are listed in the yellow pages, a multitude of possibilities are within your grasp. Become imaginative to rule yourself "capable" while looking through the phone book or internet.

Your main focus should be to establish contact, arouse interest, develop interest aroused, and consummate with a schedule interview. You might conduct a call as follows: "Hello, I'd like to speak to the personnel director. Is he/she available to talk with me. Could I have his/her name please?" Or, "Hello, I'm looking for employment and would like to speak with someone who does the hiring for the company. Could I have his/her name please?"

When you get the personnel director on the phone, this is not the time to stammer or falter. Start right in on him. Immediately introduce yourself in terms of your skills, and/or interest you have that are valued by the employer. For example, "Hello Mr. Miller, **I'm Carl Robinson, and I have experience** as a stock clerk." Your opening line should include your name and a statement of your skills and/or interest. Following that, specific questions and relevant experiences bring best results.

Such an endeavor might include your explaining of a course you've just concluded, and how excited you are to put your training to use on the job. Or, explain, for example, how you would like to learn the fast food business, from the bottom up.

Close the conversation with a short elaboration, knowing that he will at sometime have openings. Ask if you could you stop by that afternoon for a retroactive interview. Even if the potential employer is not particularly nice to you, remember to close your conversation politely. "Thank you for speaking with me." After all, either you or the potential employer might develop a mutual interest at some later time. **Don't burn bridges!**

CHAPTER SEVENTEEN

TALKING SHOP

We have many opportunities to show our knowledge of company operations. More often, these opportunities occur during daily lunch and/or other breaks. Our colleagues are more susceptible to conversations about company functions during these occasions. Use these opportunities to your promotional advantage.

An upwardly mobile employee has an intricate knowledge of company policy and procedures, product lines, and materials used. Initiate and subliminally direct conversations concerning these subjects. By reading current journals pertaining to your industry, you can become familiar with it's latest trends.

Prepare yourself to make comparisons between "old" and/or other methodology versus "new." Wherever possible, accentuate the "economically-based" procedure. One that is less time-consuming and allows for increased productivity. Company expansion is the ultimate theme here, so prepare yourself to make valid conversation.

CHAPTER EIGHTEEN

CLIMBING THE CORPORATE LADDER

For those of you who are seeking promotion from within a company, there are effective methods applicable to this situation. Foremost is having structure in your "**GAME PLAN**."

First of all, clarify in your mind the specific position and/or department you want. Set a reasonable time, in terms of months or years, in which you can vividly imagine and indeed see yourself in that position. After that, it is a succession of steps in which you watch and compare your contributions and accomplishments to those of others within the company.

A good way to initiate your approach is with a personal advertising campaign. You can start by improving your credibility among your colleagues. Substantiate the belief in others that you know what you are doing with in the company.

You want your reputation to become such that your expertise and overall knowledge of job-related intricacies is without question.

When you are given a project, let it be known that you set high standards for accomplishments, and that you use a multitude of information from reliable data to achieve success. In fact, you not only accomplish your specific project, you discover other implications relevant to company productivity.

Combine the knowledge you have of company productivity with that of current and successful trends. Again, subscribing to and reading magazines that cater to the concerns of your company will keep you abreast of current developments. Get every perspective possible and be prepared to give the pros and cons of these developments. Attending seminars and conferences in your industry will also help you in this area.

At this point, **it is relevant to reinforce** the notion that no one individual knows everything. So it is quite important to realize when to keep your mouth closed, as well as when to talk. Also, not every project is going to beam with the brilliance you want. It is your task to make the project shine. In the event you are not as successful in a project as you thought you might be, remember that everybody fails at one time or another. If this happens with your project, it is important that you salvage everything possible in terms of what you did accomplish. Be realistic with your overall conclusions, but positive in its make-up.

When communicating your ideas, know the facts of the matter. Prepare yourself to substantiate your facts with current statistics, and/or research that support your ideas. It is important that you stabilize and maintain your stature among your colleagues. Not knowing or half knowing the facts will surely raise doubt your ability. **I am sure you have the "company big-mouth" that everybody says "he doesn't know what he's talking about." One can learn a good lesson by watching his mistakes**.

If there is someone else in the company that seems to be progressing, in terms of upward mobility, you should observe that person. Pursuing a similar course of action might just as well work for you. But your hard work, will work best for you.

Have you ever noticed that many memos circulated throughout the company come from one particular employee. Most of the information contained in these memos is not new concepts, but rather reinforced old ideas. Many times such an individual is playing the "authority game," along with the concept of "self-fulfilling prophesy." The result is that of an orchestrated publicity campaign, as well.

Many times, under this circumstance, employees assume that you are already in command by "unofficial decree." If you play your cards right, the next step is only a matter of formality. If this does indeed become the case, most employees would not want to make an enemy of you. This also lends adherence to your credibility and it develops employee loyalty. If and when this is accomplished, your superiors should notice.

Gently persuade them to notice, along with the notion that you deserve higher status, and that all superiors would benefit from your having a promotion. Thus, the self-fulfilling prophesy is a realization, in that you subliminally compel superiors to want you to command.

It is important to mention here that one should not issue unauthorized memos, make promises you can't keep, or antagonize immediate superiors. They might think you are trying to get their position. This could precipitate a multitude of problems that, needless to say, could make it rough for you. In order to get your nose into the tent, you might try having memos issued by a suggestion to a higher up.

If it's a good idea you have, the superior gets credit for having the good sense to listen to a sound suggestion. If the idea doesn't work, have the understanding that it was one that was "suggested" by an employee who thought that all employees and the company would benefit from its implementation. If and when you accomplish this, you are now carrying some of the responsibility in the company's progress.

Properly document all of your suggestions via dated memorandum on company stationary. Keep a copy for use in your annual job proficiency evaluation. Ask the date of this procedure, and bring your documents. **Do not sign documents that you disagree with.** Obtain an immediate copy of all documents you have signed. If your ideas have been incorporated into company policy, use these attributes to your promotional advantage. Inform the employer of your aspirations for vertical, lateral, or salary momentum.

CHAPTER NINETEEN

COMPANY SOCIAL FUNCTIONS

Never miss the opportunity to meet a good strategically useful friend.   Employee interaction at company-sponsored social activities can provide you with such an opportunity.   One should participate with innovative enthusiasm.   For instance, if you are physically unable to play volleyball, volunteer to coach the team.   If there is a need to do so, don't forget to mention that you know nothing about the game.

Such events are often orchestrated by the company.   The concept is to encourage all employees to function as a "company family" unit. **The family that works and plays together, stays together.**   In sports and other events, your participation enhances your image as a "company team player." The position you undertake will often transcend your identity at the work place; i.e., coach or chairperson further demonstrates ones' ability in organizational skills.

This is also a measurement of your alter ego. Perhaps you've always wanted to become the coach of the entire operation or C.E.O., or "Chief." Do not burn yourself out within the company before your time. Exhibit a willingness to participate in every aspect of company enterprise. **Look to and learn from the current chief because one day you should intend to assume that position.**

At first mention of the company Christmas party, several thoughts may enter one's mind. The first one should be, **"I will not make an idiot of myself via alcohol intoxication."** Instead, why not honestly evaluate your capability as the designated driver. This is done with the utmost awareness of the **responsibility** the position incurs.

I do not wish to divert the reader's attention from the overt implication of the company social function. It is to alleviate job accumulated stress. The reader chooses the best family possible for this accomplishment. We all like to have a good time, in as many phases of our lives as possible. So have a good time at these functions. But also be mindful of the fact that **your every action,** whether you like it or not, **is being scrutinized** and can have major impact on your current status and future upward mobility in the company.

We all have integral responsibilities to our families and careers. One should develop and maintain a progressive mentality, with respect to his or her career. **You want to project to the world, most especially to your superiors, that "I am strictly business, and I have no other business but business. Let there be no doubt about it. I am a serious business person.**"

CHAPTER TWENTY

STRATEGIC QUESTIONS TO ASK THE INTERVIEWER
(And a little word to the wise!!!)

Be extremely tactful and very cautious here!   Do not go overboard asking questions in an interview.   If you must, be concise, keep them to a minimum, be intelligent, diplomatic, and most importantly, be brief. No employer likes to be put on the spot, be put under pressure themselves and have the table turned on them during an interview. You do not have to know everything at that very moment in time. Understand that the interview process is the employer's moment for questions, not yours.

It is also wise to understand that each word you utter reflects on you during your interview and can be the either a positive for you or a complete turn off for your potential employer. Given the evaluative and subjective nature of the interview process, a negative mark is easy to receive, even on a good answer. Therefore, it is absolutely critical at this juncture that you make certain your questions are well thought out. Sample questions that you may use are as follows: I strongly recommend asking no more than two during an interview.

1. What are the primary results you would like
    to see produced by me in this job?

2. Please tell me the pay range the company
    has in mind for this job?

3. What is the largest single problem facing
    your staff now, where this particular
    position is concerned?

4. Can you show me where this position fits
    into your organization?

5. What is the strengths and limitations as
    you see them for the department where I
    will be working?

CHAPTER TWENTY ONE

TOUGH QUESTIONS ASKED BY EMPLOYERS

You will want to be well prepared and have nothing short of great answers to each of the potential questions below PREPARED IN ADVANCE. Even if all of the questions are not ultimately asked, working through the answers in your head and having your **GREAT answers ready** and well though out will be a confidence building and a mental toughness exercise that will pay dividends to you long into the future. Guess what? Once you finish the tough questions below, you just might find out something new about yourself.

1. What are your long range and short range goals and objectives, when and why did you establish these goals, and how are you preparing yourself to achieve them?

2. What specific goals, other than those related to your occupations, have you established for yourself for the next 10 years?

3. What do you see yourself doing five years from now?

4. What do you really want to do in life?

5. What are your long range career objectives?

6. How do you plan to achieve your career goals?

7. What are the most important rewards you expect in your business career?

8. What do you expect to be earning in five years?

9. Why did you choose the career for which you are preparing?

10. Which is more important to you, the money or the type of job?

11. What do you consider to be your greatest strengths and weaknesses?

12. How would you describe yourself?

13. How do you think a friend or professor who knows you would describe you?

14. What motivates you to put forth your greatest efforts?

15. How has your college experience prepared you for a business career?

16. Why should I hire you?

17. What qualifications do you have that make you think that you will be successful in this business?

18. How do you determine or evaluate success?

19. What do you think it takes to be successful in a company like ours?

20. In what ways do you think you can make a contribution to our company?

21. What qualities should a successful manager posses?

22. Describe the relationship that should exist between a supervisor and those reporting to him or her.

23. What two or three accomplishments have given you the most satisfaction? Why?

24. Describe your most rewarding college experience.

25. If you were hiring a graduate for this position, what qualities would you look for?

26. Why did you select your college or university?

27. What led you to choose your field of major study?

28. What college subjects did you like best? Why?

29. What college subjects did you like least? Why?

30. If you could do so, how would you plan your academic study differently? Why?

31. What changes would you make in your college or university? Why?

32. Do you have plans for continued study? An advance degree?

33. Do you think that your grades are a good indication of your academic achievement?

34. What have you learned from participation in extra-curricular activities?

35. In what kind of a work environment are you most comfortable?

36. How do you work under pressure?

37. In what part-time or summer jobs have you been most interested? Why?

38. How would you describe the ideal job for you following graduation?

39. Why did you decide to seek a position with this company?

40. What do you know about our company?

41. What two or three things are most important to you in your job?

42. Are you seeking employment in a company of a certain size? Please explain why!

43. What criteria are you using to evaluate the company for which you hope to work?

44. Do you have a geographical preference? Why?

45. Will you relocate? Does relocation bother you.

46. Are you willing to travel?

47. Are you willing to spend at least six months as a trainee?

48. Why do you think you might like to live in the community in which our company is located?

49. What major problem have you encountered and how did you deal with it?

50. What have you learned from you mistakes?

Reprinted from the Northwestern Endicott Report by V. R. Lindquist by permission of Northwestern University Placement Center, Evanston, IL.

CHAPTER TWENTY TWO

ACTION WORDS USED TO DESCRIBE YOUR ATTRIBUTES

In successfully blowing your horn, you will want to stress accomplishments, not just duties. Another very effective tool is to describe these accomplishments or duties with powerful action verbs. The strategic use of words ending in -ing or –ed can prove to be a very useful technique.

1. FUNCTIONAL (TRANSFERABLE) SKILLS – these are those that you can take with you from job to job.

Some examples that you can use are:

accomplished,	demonstrated,	instructed
processed	advised	designed
interpreted	produced	administered
determined	invented	proved

analyzed	developed	investigated
provided	approved	directed
launched	recommended	arranged
documented	lead	reduced
assisted	eliminated	maintained
re-evaluated	assembled	engineered
managed	researched	attained
established	maximized	reviewed
built	evaluated	modified
revised	communicated	expanded
monitored	saved	completed
expedited	motivated	scheduled
composed	facilitated	negotiated
selected	computed	founded
observed	sold	conceived
generated	organized	solved

conducted	guided	originated
stimulated	controlled	identified
optimized	stream-lines	coordinated
implemented	performed	structured
created	improved	planned
supervised	decreased	increased
prepared	taught/trained	delegated
influenced	presented	translated
delivered	initiated	problem-solved

2. **ADAPTIVE SKILLS** – these skills are personal traits and may be best defined as those that describe you. Some examples are:

active	diplomatic	innovative	practical
adaptable	disciplined	instrumental	productive
adept	efficient	logical	reliable
broad-minded	energetic	methodical	resourceful

conscientious	enterprising	objective	self-reliant
creative	experienced	participation	sensitive
dependable	firm	personable	successful
determined	honest	positive	tactful

CHAPTER
TWENTY THREE

RESUME RECORD

Keeping a resume record can prove to be an invaluable asset to you. You will want have a readily available listing of all employment efforts you have made, regardless of whether they were failures or a success. You never know when you may need to go back and draw on these sources and employment contacts. Below is an example of how this record can be recorded.

Date Sent	Employer, Individual Contacted	Date Replied	Comments
___	_____	_____	_____
___	_____	_____	_____
___	_____	_____	_____
___	_____	_____	_____

FURTHER REFERENCES

Re-Entering.
by Eleanor Berman

From Kitchen to Career.
　　by Shirley Sloan Fader

**How To Get Work When Your Husband Is
Against It, Your Children Aren't Old Enough and
There's Nothing You Can Do Anyhow.**
　　by Schwartz, Schiner and Gillotti

The Job Sharing Handbook.
　　by Barney Olmsted and Suzanne Smith

Writing That Works
　　by Oliu, Brusaw and Palved

Written in loving memory
of

Mrs. Inez Moreland.

Special thanks also to
Mr. & Mrs. Wilmer "Buddy" Morris.

This book was written By Bruce Edward Beal.

Initial Editing by:
Mrs. Nancy Perkins
Reconcilers Fellowship
Jackson, MS
And final edit done by the
ZWORLD-NET PUBLISHING STAFF

ABOUT THE AUTHOR:

BRUCE EDWARD BEAL was born in Jackson Mississippi. He graduated from Brinkley High School and from there matriculated and graduated from Jackson State University, earning a Bachelor of Science Degree in Psychiatry. He feels his past and what brought him to his life work (of helping others) is not important. He only wants to be of service to his fellow man.

Professor Beal has written numerous documents on the subject of employment. Professor Beal has been recognized throughout America as an outstanding resource on the topic of employment. His exceptional efforts have aided many across America in their QUEST TO OBTAIN THAT ELUSIVE HIGHER PAYING JOB.

ZWORLD-NET PUBLISHING INC.

THE POWER OF THE WRITTEN WORD!!!

BRUCE EDWARD BEAL

HOW TO GET
THAT
HIGHER
PAYING JOB
BY
BRUCE EDWARD
BEAL

AN IMPRINT OF
ZWORLDNET PUBLISHING INC.
ISBN 09712310-9-5 //// A SPECIAL EDITION

HOW TO GET
THAT
HIGHER
PAYING JOB

****

BY
BRUCE
EDWARD BEAL

****

****

*

***

THIS NON-FICTIONAL BOOK IS A PRODUCT OF

<<<>>>

ZWORLD-NET PUBLISHING INC.

<<<<>>>>

THE POWER OF THE WRITTEN WORD!!!

<<<>>>

HOW TO GET THAT

HIGHER

PAYING JOB

BY

BRUCE EDWARD BEAL

**AN IMPRINT OF
ZWORLDNET PUBLISHING INC.**
ISBN 0-9712310-9-5 //// A SPECIAL LARGE PRINT EDITION

HOW TO GET THAT HIGHER PAYING JOB

THE HOLY

GRAIL

OF

EMPLOYMENT

BOOKS

HOW TO GET THAT HIGHER PAYING JOB

THIS NON-FICTIONAL BOOK IS A PRODUCT OF

<<<>>>

ZWORLD-NET PUBLISHING INC.

<<<<>>>

THE POWER OF THE WRITTEN WORD!!!

<<<>>>

HOW TO GET THAT HIGHER PAYING JOB

THIS NON-FICTIONAL BOOK IS A PRODUCT OF

<<<>>>

ZWORLD-NET PUBLISHING INC.

<<<<>>>>

THE POWER OF THE WRITTEN WORD!!!

<<<>>>

HOW TO GET THAT

HIGHER

PAYING JOB

BY

BRUCE EDWARD BEAL

AN IMPRINT OF
ZWORLDNET PUBLISHING INC.
ISBN 0-9712310-9-5 //// A SPECIAL EDITION